P9-EDU-701

SHABBY CHIC INTERIORS

CALGARY PUBLIC LIBRARY

OCT   2012

RACHEL ASHWELL
SHABBY CHIC
INTERIORS

MY ROOMS, TREASURES, AND TRINKETS

PHOTOGRAPHY BY AMY NEUNSINGER

CICO BOOKS
LONDON NEW YORK

First edition published in 2009 by CICO Books
This edition published in 2012 by CICO Books
An imprint of
Ryland Peters & Small
20–21 Jockey's Fields   519 Broadway, 5th Floor
London WC1R 4BW   New York, NY 10012

10 9 8 7 6 5 4 3 2 1

Text © Rachel Ashwell 2009, 2012
Design and photography © CICO Books 2009, 2012

The author's moral rights have been asserted.
All rights reserved. No part of this publication
may be reproduced, stored in a retrieval system, or
transmitted in any form or by any means, electronic,
mechanical, photocopying, or otherwise, without
the prior permission of the publisher.

A CIP catalog record for this book is available from
the Library of Congress and the British Library.

ISBN 978 1 908170 80 4

Printed in China

Text: Alexandra Parsons
Design: Roger Hammond
Design concept: Jennifer De Klaver
Photographer: Amy Neunsinger
(photographs on pages 40–41, 44, and 52 by
Miguel Flores Vianna; photographs on pages 131
and 132 by Ngoc Minh Ngo)

CONTENTS

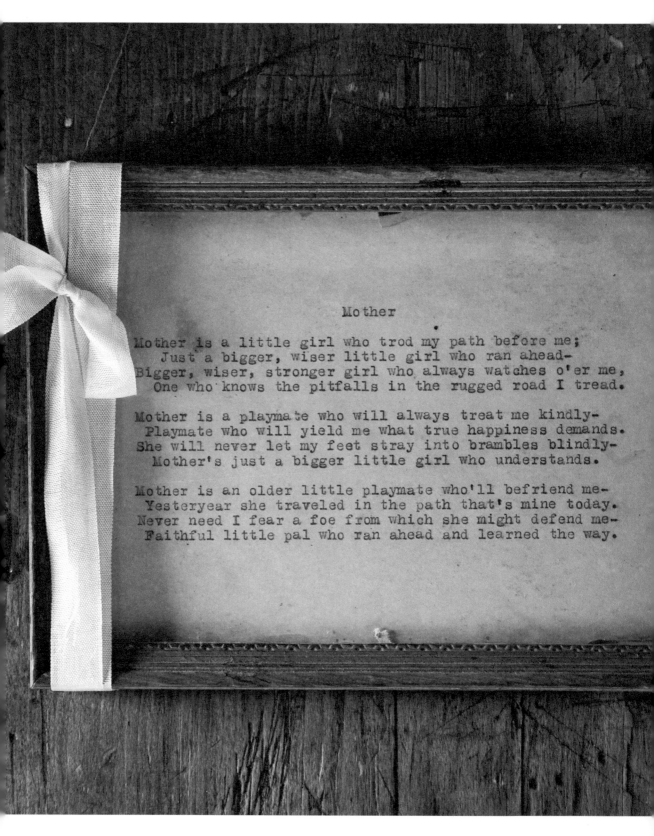

Mother

Mother is a little girl who trod my path before me;
    Just a bigger, wiser little girl who ran ahead-
Bigger, wiser, stronger girl who always watches o'er me,
    One who knows the pitfalls in the rugged road I tread.

Mother is a playmate who will always treat me kindly-
    Playmate who will yield me what true happiness demands.
She will never let my feet stray into brambles blindly-
    Mother's just a bigger little girl who understands.

Mother is an older little playmate who'll befriend me-
    Yesteryear she traveled in the path that's mine today.
Never need I fear a foe from which she might defend me-
    Faithful little pal who ran ahead and learned the way.

Dedication

To Mum, 1927–2008

With thanks

To Lily and Jake. People say we don't choose our family. But Jake and Lily have grown into people I would choose as friends. Interesting and interested, responsible, compassionate, loving, and funny.

To my dad and my sister as we find our way.

This book was created during a major crossroads in my life. Unwavering friends stood strongly and consistently by my side. You made it easy to recognize what authentic friendship truly is. You know who you are, and I appreciate you all so very much.

To Judith, my previous publisher, who led the way to my world of books.

To Cindy and David at Cico Books who stuck with me during some uncertain times. To Sally, Roger, Alex, and Gillian, who let me sit on their shoulders.

To dear Amy. Our fourth book together. We have an unspoken language. This was a special time together. Thank you, your wonderful team, and Carol for supporting us.

To Lupe, for eyelashes, lunch, and for always knowing where everything is.

And thanks to all looking at this book. Likely you are one of the many who have supported me over the years, as a customer, a supplier of goods, an employee, or a lover of Shabby Chic. We created something quite wonderful, together. This book is for us all.

INTRODUCTION

Home truly is where we hang our hats, and I have hung my hats in a lot of different places. To move as often as I have is not so unusual in today's world. The acceptance that nothing lasts forever should not deter from making an experience as wonderful as it can be, during its time. When I move into a home, I never quite know my length of stay but "home is where the heart is" are the truest of words. My philosophy is that wherever I am, I make my nest, even in a rented home or hotel. With flowers, music, candles, and beautiful, comfortable, and functional things, a home will be that much lovelier a place for our hearts to be.

This book is about my favorite interiors, treasures, and trinkets, a true compilation of the world of Rachel Ashwell Shabby Chic. It is my attempt to portray the qualities of beauty, comfort, and function. The diversity of homes in this book range from the pure whiteness of my beach house, to a modern canyon loft, to a bohemian, eclectic townhouse, but each one in its way resonates with my design philosophy. Each and every time I move, it gives me the opportunity to tweak my style. As an artist it is necessary to evolve. I have had the pleasure of having a career of beauty and very little passes through my design world that isn't pure eye candy. Sometimes just owning treasures is enough for me, I enjoy them for a while, take away some inspiration, and then pass them on to someone

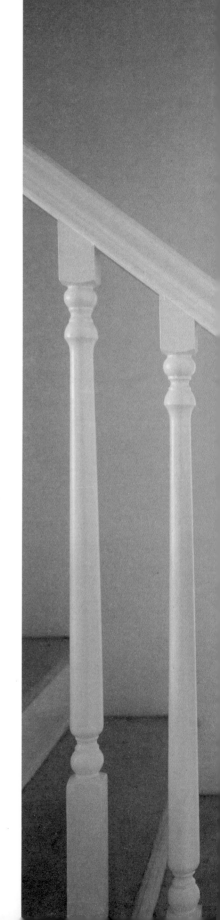

else. But there are a few chosen pieces that I consider "forever to keep": the quintessential classic, the perfect patina, or the perfectly functional practical piece, these are the elements of forever. But I do not only treasure star pieces. Equal in importance for me are the details, the bits and pieces that take the supporting and understudy roles which are vital when it comes to creating a complete story. And finding and compiling these takes time—it takes editing, it takes research, but it separates magic from mediocrity. And it creates soul.

I have always valued my source of inspiration. Sometimes the ideas born from inspiration find their way effortlessly into my design, my values, and how I live my life. I never had any formal training in anything, life has been my school. My biggest source of inspiration was my mum, who used to collect, restore, and sell antique dolls. She had drawers, cupboards, paper bags, cardboard boxes, and tins, filled with glass eyes, little wigs, and unwound wire hangers to restring their arms which were all rather scary. But what was glorious to me were the mounds of tattered ribbons, crumpled scrap fabrics, stained laces, salvaged sleeves or collars from Victorian clothing beyond repair, and lots of little buttons and smooshed fabric flowers. While others in her profession restored to perfection, she embraced the subtle signs of a doll worn by love, and restored them by honoring their character. In doing so she was my teacher; I learned by observing and letting her essence become mine. I remember her work-worn hands, always with a thimble and sewing threads. I remember her painstakingly editing bits and bobs that were suitable to tell her story. I remember the powdered dyes of pale pink, blues, and greens she used to quietly create her magic. This would become my palette. She knew every stitch and scrap might be missed by many, but would be appreciated by anyone who noticed her "beauty of imperfection."

As years went by, Mum got involved in other interests. But her values of accepting things the way they were, were demonstrated in most everything she did. She always had time for people and she would listen—she offered opinions when asked, but never judged. She allowed us all to beat to our own drums. She only took on projects that she could take care of herself, she didn't delegate the living of her own life. Her garden was purposely teeny, as that was what she could maintain herself. She made her mark quietly and took up little space in this world.

When she passed away this year, I gathered up all her treasured bits and bobs. I am enjoying the process of looking at each and every piece and feeling close to her, for I understand the beauty in the tattered, thanks to her. And so for all I learned, and for all I have passed on, it was all thanks to Mum.

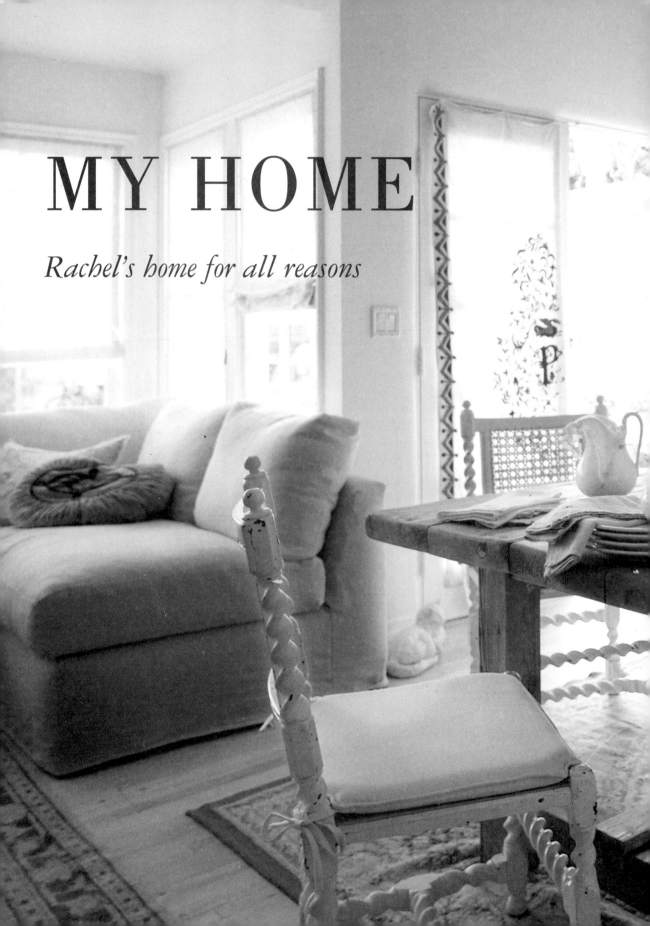

MY HOME

Rachel's home for all reasons

The everything room is a chameleon (*previous page*), transforming from a room of twinkling crystal elegance to a workplace of bohemian artistic activity. My dose of New York loft-style living inspired me to open up the ground floor. My design has evolved, allowing the pretty and the tough to bring out the best in each other—hence the petal-pink linen and dancing chandeliers teamed with dark solid woods and grubby taupe linens.

A chandelier is quintessential to my decorating (*opposite*). Heavy crystal teardrops hang from delicate, sparingly strung strings of crystal beads. I hung this low over my table to embrace its presence, but its airy design does not obstruct dinner conversation.

This rack originally housed bits and pieces for making shoes (*left*). Except for some permanently stuck-on goopey glue, it cleaned up well and now serves a new purpose, housing vintage plates, pinnies, and pretty things.

My nest

I have often thought myself like a bird, gathering my belongings and setting up a home of beauty, comfort, and function. For the last twenty years the anchor for my decisions has been my children, Jake and Lily. I have always supported independence in my children, but I am also a big believer that strength and adventure come from a sense of belonging, so that was a priority for me. As Jake and Lily left home for college, my new consideration was how best I could create a home that could sit comfortably whether empty, or filled with family and friends. I had seen this house some time ago, in its original unrestored 1920s state, and something about it felt it could be my "everything I need" house. Occasionally I would drive by to check on its evolution until one day I popped a note through the door to see if I could buy it. It turned out the new owner was wanting a fancier house and even though he had just completed a makeover to bring in glitz and bling, it hadn't quite worked, and he was happy to sell. So then I began the curious mission of "unrestoring": heaving out brand-new kitchen cabinets and deluxe whirlpool baths until I got back to the authentic and real.

(*clockwise from top*) A farmhouse jug gets a little frill with a ruffled lace and rhinestone fly cover. A watercolor of Van Morrison by my daughter layers quietly behind my pretty mum. Keep the faith candle—words to remember, always. A vintage table with fabulous original paint and lovely little wheels acts as the preparation island; often a floating stool nearby is pulled over for a friend to sit and chat.

One could say this is a wasted space for such a grand little chandelier (*right*), but it's often the smallest detail that makes the biggest statement. The randomly planked ceiling was a pleasant surprise. Previously hidden underneath plasterboard, the strips of wood are a little wonky, but perfect.

The everything room

All rooms lead into this room designed for everything. A twelve-foot table is the centerpiece. While lovely to have for the reunion part of my life, during thequieter days, the table could have been a bit oversized, but once I stopped calling it a dining table, it took on the role of the core of activity from dinner parties to a corner for a cup of tea, to laying out art projects that need to lie around rather than be put away. My lovely petal-pink linen sectional sofa with mushy cushions welcomes movie-watching and napping. The velvet pillow has the perfect amount of stuffing to its flop. It is a beautiful room with a good balance between the feminine and the bold. It is pretty without being cluttered but I do embrace a lived-in house—chipped and worn-in takes the edge off being the one to break the perfection. Texture and faded muted colors create the tapestry of this room. Teal and beige evolved to be the theme palette, mainly shown in the mixture of threadbare and faded flea-market rugs. The slubby vintage linen curtains are worthy of a little café rod but, for now, push pins hold them in place. I have dabbled in feng shui from time to time, but I think the flow and feel of a house is intuitive. This room owns the central space and the furnishings found their places instinctively. The light travels around the room, with magical morning light and evening light of total peace. This is home, for now.

(*previous page*) I got the idea for the diagonal tiling and two-inch marble inlay from an old dairy, and I think it inherits the association of the cool, calm, and caring ways of preparing food.

Lovely things to look at (*clockwise from top left*). On the corner of a shelf sit a vintage tea caddy, a fancy egg cup, and a glass with inspiring words. A pair of delicate botanical watercolors are thumb-tacked to the window. The Florentine trays add muted color to the old dresser. The pantry cupboard is a vintage find. The little bit of frippery hanging from the knob is there because it's there.

It took me a long time to find the perfect kitchen faucet (*right*). It is nickel-plated with a lovely patina, more subdued than chrome.

Kitchen

Authentic is the way I would describe my kitchen. I won a couple of popularity contests with my construction team the day I removed all the recently installed slick modern storage units and countertops. While I have affections for squeaky cupboards, wonky drawers, and dripping faucets, the reality is that every kitchen needs careful planning and to function well. I removed most of the cupboards and installed a couple of open shelves, my philosophy being that if you don't use it, lose it, and if I can't see it, I forget I have it, so all my new and vintage dinnerware and odd useful charming things end up for daily use, not always as originally intended, but used nonetheless. The countertops are of pure white Thasos marble honed to take off the shine and straight-edged—any bevel would have been too fancy. A rough wood dresser houses a multitude of things, and baskets sit underneath, storing essentials. On top, a microwave and books rumble together in orderly chaos. Farmhouse sinks to me are a must for any home that can house one, and I love how they bring instant cottage or castle to the story. Pots and pans and cleaning things are actually hidden away in unsqueaky drawers under the countertop, concealed by crudely constructed rough wood doors. I pride myself on having little clutter, however every room gets one "junk drawer" and the kitchen is no exception—receipts, bottle caps, and matchbooks roam around until clean-out day.

There's not much room for furniture in a nook (*opposite*). This folk dresser, painted an unusual aqua, nestles perfectly into its niche.

Pretty dishes and interesting vintage silverware (*left*) make washing dishes a pleasure.

My inspirational office (*overleaf*) opens into the kitchen.

The nook

I just love a nook. It's the unsung hero, providing a vital transition between one place and another—a little space that deserves a lot of respect through an offering of candles or of flowers. This nook joins the kitchen to the downstairs bathroom and guest room so it is a well-trodden path. As with any small space, this nook was the perfect opportunity to use leftover rolls of vintage wallpaper. My irritated but patient wallpaper-hanger was not happy with the wonky joins, but vintage wallpaper needs to have glue applied and the paper is brittle to the touch so imperfections are inevitable—embraced by me, but hard for a professional to accept. This wallpaper made the space a real flower bower, where I always put a pitcher of flowers, preferably pink.

(*clockwise from left*) The skirt that never got to the ball. Art by happenstance was created when I hung this tulle petticoat on a rod. It's been there beautifully and endlessly admired ever since. My girly pen pot—chipped, but much loved. The chair was originally from the Time Life Building in New York. The white leather was a bit slippery to sit on, hence the Indian cushion that gives both traction and mush (that's comfort to me).

A Florentine paper holder (*top right*) makes a colorful receptacle for outdated papers and vital reminders. Lovely journals cherished by my mum and now by me (*bottom*).

My office at home

My home office started life as a breakfast room, the cozy proximity of the kitchen is perfect for multitasking. And for teatime. Other than a couple of pale blue painted harvest tables, a white leather chair, and breezy voile curtains hung on a set of French doors, everything else in the room evolves and changes as my projects command. Fortunately everything that pops in is usually so lovely in some form or another that process and mess always look beautiful. Behind my desk is a memo board that's an ever-evolving work of art. Cards made by my children share equal status with my bits and bobs and dates to remember, mainly already past.

Pretty clothes I likely won't wear but enjoy to see hang (*right*): a nearly-worn wedding dress, a clown costume, and a collection of unrestored prom dresses create loveliness. To create some overflow storage I placed a sizeable robin's egg blue vintage cabinet. Office papers and my stock of candles are stored there.

The sofa and the fireplace anchors lots of floppy pink accent (*overleaf*). Me daydreaming.

The hodgepodge room

This room could easily have been the forgotten space or the walk-through room at best, had it not been the recipient of a misplaced but much appreciated fireplace more suited to a drafty castle than my sunny Californian home. But nonetheless, its presence gave the room the upper hand over its sister room where the television and the kitchen sit. I have always loved dark brown leather Chesterfield sofas but never had the right home. Finally this seemed right. However, I did change the leather set of cushions for sage velvet so I still had elements of my mushy comfort. The shallow but densely strung and clustered crystal chandelier hangs low over the coffee table. Dimly lit, with candles and the fire, it is nearly impossible not to have a romantic moment. I have allowed the room to evolve and find its use. While the sofa and fire are the focus, the back part of the room often becomes a spontaneous overflow from the surrounding rooms. It randomly acquired a chair and objects that are on their way somewhere else—all in all, a bit of a hodgepodge.

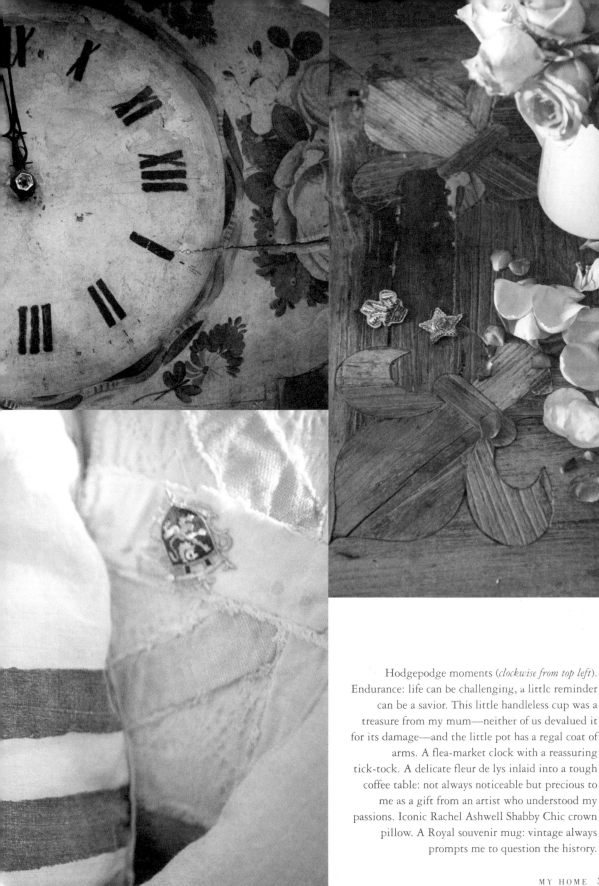

Hodgepodge moments (*clockwise from top left*). Endurance: life can be challenging, a little reminder can be a savior. This little handleless cup was a treasure from my mum—neither of us devalued it for its damage—and the little pot has a regal coat of arms. A flea-market clock with a reassuring tick-tock. A delicate fleur de lys inlaid into a tough coffee table: not always noticeable but precious to me as a gift from an artist who understood my passions. Iconic Rachel Ashwell Shabby Chic crown pillow. A Royal souvenir mug: vintage always prompts me to question the history.

(*clockwise from top left*) A vintage First Communion veil, both pretty and spiritual. A vintage candelabra with luscious lavender crystal drops. Ranunculuses are my favorite flower—an unsung rose with petals that that develop a lovely tissue character as they age. I buy them in abundance. Sitting on a chair, enjoying their moment to fuel my inspiration, a pair of theatrical crowns, still with the price tag.

A basketful of my heritage (*opposite*). Stars and stripes and the Union Jack celebrate my dual British and American citizenships. Flowers, pearls, lace, and feathers layer in my own individual identity.

Many wonderful objects pass through my hands. Sometimes just owning them for a short time is all I need and sometimes they stay to become a source of inspiration. I do like them easily visible as at different moments I see different qualities. My eye is consistent, but always evolving. My signature palette of pastels is now enriched with gold, purples, faded deep colors, and dark wood. I find beauty in religious and royal iconography but I also like the association these symbols inherit from faith and belief.

Beautiful boudoir

I am just as happy in a beach shack or a barn in the fields of Texas; however, when I want the classical, luxurious hotel experience I am often left disappointed with corporate luxury. This bedroom was my stage to create the Grand Hotel that I have yet to find: a place to play out my imaginings of being a princess. Decadent plush silks, velvets, and crumpled linens were my vision. To me, a test of lovely bedding is if the bed looks equally yummy unmade. A vital glamour element is vintage lighting: chandeliers, wall sconces, and lampshades (often tattered) make the story real.

My glamorous bedroom (*above*) is rumpled with layers of linen, silks, and cashmere. A tufted velvet headboard has become my signature piece.

The transition from bedroom to bathroom is my makeup area (*opposite*). Typical to me, a quiet, tired little chair keeps the balance shabby and chic.

My chandelier (*overleaf*) has blue crystal drops to enhance other blue accents. Mix-and-match nightstands take the edge off perfection.

"Mere colour can speak to the soul
in a thousand different ways."

Oscar Wilde

Dressing room

My one deviation from my aversion to built-ins is here in my dressing room. Fancy shelves and closets with mirrors and tie hooks lined every wall. Very practical probably, but once again I asked my friendly builder if he would rip them out and replace with wonky cupboards. The doors are not aligned and barely close, but somehow they seem better matched to my jeans and cowboy boots, although I do add some bling to my wardrobe with gold shoes and bags. This room is somewhat incomplete, but the disregard of beauty is quite magical.

(*clockwise from top left*) A perfect pink touch in my bedroom. A regal presence in my makeup area: I pop my hairclips in his back pouch. My choice of footwear speaks for itself. I decided on brass filigree hardware on the doors to my dressing room cupboards, glass or wood wouldn't give me the regal fuss I wanted.

Because I feel my dress code is undeserving of a dressing room, I never quite finished this room (*above*). While the Victorian lace curtains are divine, they are casually pinned to the window frame. The lovely regal wallpaper is counterbalanced by the scruffy pale blue table.

(*previous page*) Luscious detail of an elegant Florentine cabinet. I had never seen one before with a pink accent, usually they are more jewel tones. The gold brings out the glamour of the silvery-pink curtains, decadent in their fullness. I love all aspects of ballet, this charcoal and pastel is a lovely choice of medium to keep her out of the frilly zone. Other bits and bobs get placed here over time.

Details from my bathroom (*below and right*). I specified a rubber bath plug and a white rubber protector for the showerhead (changed from black). A nightie hangs on the door and there are always flowers.

(*overleaf*) The tattily opulent sconces and mirror were a long search. The little pink tag hanging off the lace curtain surrounded by the chunky marble is poetry to my eyes.

My Grand Hotel bathroom

As understated as my glamorous bathroom is, I paid much attention to researching the subtle proportions and detail. The marble slabs on the walls were more expensive than tiles, but as the bathroom was small, it seemed an affordable extravagance. I love the strong detail of the bullnose chair rail and the proper Grand Hotel heated towel rack, which is beautiful and functional and adds immeasurably to my comfort. I had to remove a fancy whirlpool bath and it took me ages to find a modest, self-faced bath with just enough of a rim to make space for a couple of candles. It is small, but it feels authentic and it takes a lot less water to fill. Proportionally, it was going to look a little low, so I built up a platform to give it a sense of importance.

FINE DESIGN

RACHEL ASHWELL®

SHABBY CHIC®

COUTURE

Lily's room is a collapsed heap of prettiness: bohemian meets washed-out-florals. On the bed are dented pillows and abundant layers of embroidered linen, velvet, and lace, all beautifully rumpled, crumpled, and mushed.

Lily's retreat

No matter how far and wide my children and I travel, I always want there to be somewhere we call home. By the time I decorated this house Lily had left home for college. She requested that this room be colorful and flowery which I think is her way of having a little girl's room to retreat to, or maybe she had had enough white. My translation of color was to have bright colors but subdued in palette—dusty, smudgy, and overdyed. The idea of empty rooms, abandoned for months on end, is not appealing to me. So at times Lily's room doubles up as a guest room. The room is small, with a vaulted, plastered ceiling that I painted with shiny gloss paint for a cozy yet breezy look and of course the shine reflects the colored crystals in the pretty chandelier. There's a quirky little window behind the bed. It's actually completely crooked—just one of the precious off-beat proportions that so endeared the house to me.

(*clockwise from left*) Lily is studying fashion design and this is one of her inspirations, a vintage sequinned dress. Lily's pointe shoes—timeless and so personal. Tradition gone colorful in the multicolored chandelier. One of Lily's fashion sketches. A regal touch: a 1911 souvenir plate commemorating the marriage of Queen Mary and King George V. The patina is just beautiful. Princess Diana wedding glass from my Royalty collection.

Faded fabric on an old chair with a pattern
that is barely there (*right*) given a bit of
edge by a tattered denim skirt.

Shoes full of character (*below*) in an alcove
papered with vintage wallpaper.

Flowers, lace, and worn shoes

There is evidence in Lily's room of life lived to its fullest within the parameters of pretty and pink. It is an unconscious montage of the personality of a girl with a true interest in fashion who wears clothes and shoes until they fall apart, who loves faded florals and dog-eared books, and isn't too precious to splatter paint on her shoes. There were times Lily expressed the wish to stay in one house so all memories could be contained. But she has learned to travel with her memories. In the three or four years since Lily first left home for the world of college dorms and shared apartments, she has re-created this feeling wherever she lives with her portable bits and pieces. This is her reality.

Lace curtains hang on a café rod (*opposite*), the mirror leaning casually on the porcelain shelf has a pretty scalloped edge. Some metal drawers on wheels (*below*)—nothing too permanent. The vintage light socket (*below right*), complete with pull chain, has a $10 glass shade from the local hardware store.

Jake and Lily's bathroom

A utilitarian bathroom with a touch of vintage whimsy. There are no built-in cupboards as I like the eclectic feel of freestanding, one-of-a-kind cabinets that have had a life here or there. Having things out in the open forces a discipline of keeping only what you need. The subway tiles are an affordable classic, the large freestanding sink has nickel-plated repro vintage faucets, and a little seaside landscape is just there.

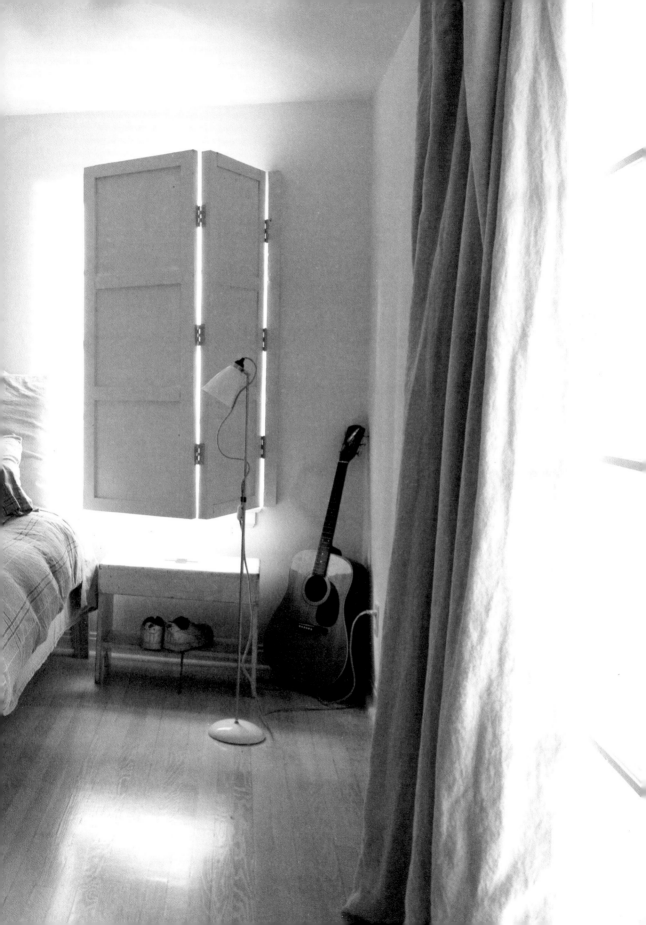

(*previous page*) With a muted palette of soft blues and creams, this room is a basic, functional, masculine comfort zone. Jake often requested black-out shades—a typical guy thing—so I had these shutters made. As it happens he'll probably get the shades he wanted behind the light-leaking shutters.

Jake's night table (*right*) is yet another found object with a bold red cross statement. The next best thing to a naked light bulb: a vintage canopy (far right), chain, and fitting with a pressed glass shade that I found on the internet. When buying vintage ceiling-hung light fittings, always try and get one with the original canopy.

(*opposite*) A funky table and chair. Voila!

Jake's space

My son has recently gone to college in New York, taking most of his stuff with him. Jake has grown up surrounded by beauty, function, and squashy comfort and also a whole lot of florals and pink—which obviously have no place in his space. He is big on comfort but not big on bedmaking, but that is okay with me. His simple wooden bed is layered with flannel, cashmere, and cotton jersey and the windows have functional, basic gray-painted shutters—very unfussy— a male take on the Shabby Chic philosophy. As for lighting (I guess fearing a chandelier), he wanted a naked lightbulb hanging from the ceiling. He got a vintage fixture that is the nearest I could bring myself to fulfilling his request. But I did sneak in an edgy floral rug. His room suits him. As long as his eyes rest on calmness, he's a wheel that doesn't squeak.

The "unrestored" stairway (*left*) leads to my linen cupboard (*opposite*). I had one roll of pretty blue floral vintage wallpaper, so I used it here. I like a bit of mismatched order and get great pleasure from my eclectic mix of bedding. The cupboard is not jammed full because I am good at letting things go and moving on. No bed needs more than a couple of changes of linen.

The top of the stairs

Landings speak of homes that were built when there was space for space. I love having a landing that is a transition space with room for things that have no place elsewhere. As part of my "unrestoring" of this house, I replaced a harsh black metal handrail with a traditional painted wood, stripped the steps, and painted the risers. At the top of my stairs is a linen cupboard, perfectly practical and pretty. Further along the landing, which leads to the bedrooms, is a favorite, authentic Shabby Chic dressing table that has inspired many people to create their own versions of the style. The original sits on the landing only because it was on the way to Lily's room, but wouldn't fit. And there it stayed. I always pay attention to where things end up by happenstance, because it may be the place they were always meant to be.

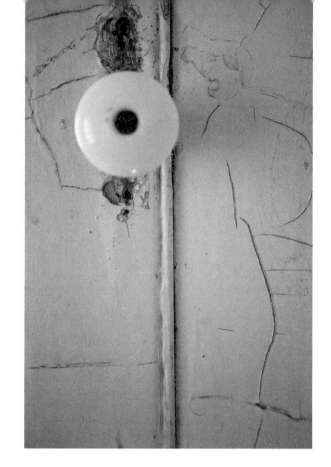

(*previous page*) The original Shabby Chic vanity piece with its perfect molding and delicious patina. The unglazed vase is a favorite piece —its shape and patina make it barely noticeable, allowing the flowers to do what they have to do. Sometimes flowers shouldn't have to compete with their container.

While I am happy with the function of the towel rack (*opposite*), it is a little shiny, so I will continue my search for an old wooden or enamel one. That's the thing with authentic, detailed restoration—some things take time to find. I am reluctantly becoming a fan of the soap pump, especially in guest bathrooms. Rather that than soaps sitting in slushy goop. My patient plumber switched the new handles on my faucets to lovely old porcelain crossbars.

The pink medicine cabinet I found years ago, knowing one day I would find a home for it. It's the perfect pink, not coral or salmon. Beautifully battered, its imperfections take it out of the pretty-pretty pink spectrum. It scrubbed up to my hygienic standards and I was able to keep the fabulous white porcelain knob (*right*).

The bathroom downstairs

I wasn't looking for glamour in this spare bathroom but I was going for authentic. The key for me to "unrestoring" this bathroom was to find vintage tiles, which have subtleties of imperfection that are impossible to reproduce. The wall tiles have the perfect amount of hairline cracks (a couple were more streaks than cracks and those were installed in the least visible places). The floor needed authenticity too. I did initially find some beautiful reclaimed French floor tiles. The sample I received was a lovely off-white with pale gray damask-type pattern. Sadly, when the very heavy boxes of the additional 200 tiles arrived, some of the off-white was cream and some of the gray was black and what was worse, they arrived while I was away and therefore got installed. The poor proud tiler had to reclaim the tiles once again. (I now have table coasters to use as gifts for quite some time.) In the end I used small hexagonal Carrara marble floor tiles, which have a timeless feel and work wonderfully with the wall tiles.

(*clockwise from left*) Even the humblest of rooms should be rewarded with favorite pieces, and this denim blue and pink rose painting for me is just that. The curtain is temporary—a torn piece of fabric just folded over a café rod. A ceiling-mounted fixture with crystal flair. In my restoration frenzy, I forgot to instal a toilet-paper holder, but these are fine where they landed up. Pierrot the clown—the character of this one has a touch of the hopeless romantic.

A pretty vintage mirror with scalloped edges, etched flowers, and a floppy bow: the epitome of tattered elegance (*left*). Over the last few years I have learned to identify my style within the context of Asian art. This piece—the contemplative, traditional figure holding a little pearl—is a prime example. It is an unusual palette for Asian art which tends more toward brighter colors, but it is my palette.

The bedding collection used here (*opposite*) is inspired by the tiny washed-out prints and ruffles of 1940s lingerie. I used dress fabrics rather than the larger-scale prints used for sheeting, so it looks like bedding made from lovely worn vintage frocks and petticoats.

Friends to stay

Until I realize my ultimate dream of owning a hotel, I will practice my skills on my guests. A guest room is a challenge to get right. It needs to be personal, but not too much, and have a character that is not too overwhelming. I like to select special things, books, candles, quietly inspirational pieces of art, that often start conversations over breakfast. I enjoy the nurturing process of making the room as comfy as possible, for someone I care about. The room is accessed through the nook, and past the bathroom, so it is tucked away from the rest of the house. It was the laundry room, but as I haven't gotten comfortable with a dressing room just for jeans and a makeup area just for lip gloss, a room just to wash clothes seemed not right (my washer and dryer are now in a cupboard under the stairs). Now this is a calm space, with my welcoming mismatched bedding, interesting vintage finds, and a chandelier that still has the price tag hanging off it.

The beautiful barn

I have always dreamed of living on a farm, so it should come as no surprise that I built a barn out back. It is a very simple, traditional, basic construction, not insulated, as this is Southern California, built from white-painted timber siding with windows from the salvage yard and basic doors with the simplest of closures. The barn is ideal for spontaneous sleepovers, for guests who don't want to leave, and as an overflow for my work space. I love how the various sources of high- and low-level crosslight flood through the barn, creating an ethereal atmosphere, similar to being in a cathedral.

A well-loved scruffy wooden bench perched outside (*above left*). The double doors open wide to create an inside/outside space.

The inside (*above right*) is as simple as the outside. No chandeliers: utilitarian metal factory light fixtures hang from the rafters. The Dutch doors are perfectly in keeping. The battered pale blue wooden trunk holds supplies of bedding and towels.

My barn is a comfortable space with a relaxed palette of natural earth tones and touches of sun-bleached blue. It is one big space with several beds, which are just very basic wooden frames with linen slipcovers that are often wheeled outside on a warm night to look at the holes in the sky. Part of the room is sectioned off with a white denim grommeted curtain hanging on a simple metal pole that hides away any elements of work that may have crept in from my office. But should I feel inspired, I can just as easily sweep open the curtains and take over the entire space as a workroom. I designed the barn for very simple upkeep. I sealed the cement floor and there aren't any rugs to worry about, stuff is contained in baskets, and the bedding just gets shaken outside for an airing.

(*previous page*) Ceiling fans are such a timeless element, and there's something rather sensual about them. I kept the fabrics neutral in tone, but texture is created with cable-knit throws, slubby linen, and pale blue cotton prints. I chose classic skeleton key locks and fat simple porcelain handles.

The beds are piled with relaxed jumbles of pillows, throws, duvets, and bolsters (*opposite*). The denim curtain divides so light pours through from the window.

The movie Mamma Mia! inspired me to paint the cement bathroom walls blue (*left*). A pink flower, a battered stool, and a fleur de lys on a piece of stained glass—I love them all. The hooks on the door substitute for storage.

In true barn-like fashion (*opposite*), the wooden slats sometimes have gaps, I love that it's not perfect. The shower curtain is lace with a plastic liner. In such a small space it is nice to observe texture; the bench is the perfect palette of worn-away blues and reds.

On the wall (*right*) is a vintage mirror. The little sink has an integral shelf, as there are no other shelves, and no cupboards.

The irregular plaster niches in the walk-in shower (*below*) were an idea I got from a magazine. Flowers last forever in a bathroom, hence in this tiny space there are four floral moments. And there's me, putting the pillows away.

The barn is such a flexible space. Nothing can come to any harm, nothing is precious, and nothing is permanent. Big double doors open invitingly with hardly a threshold to bar your way, except a piece of gravel or two that might slip through.

A perfect spot for tea parties (*right*). The ruffled rose-covered tablecloth is an old curtain that has followed me round forever.

Ranunculuses in my bird bath where hummingbirds primp and sip (*below left*). I have an eclectic collection of mismatched vintage tea sets, ever evolving (*below right*).

Gravel and roses out back

My garden is a work in progress. In time, the garden will mature and bloom. Until then, I will make do with promising buds, an appreciation of the irregular wonky stucco wall, and the pretty roses on my favorite tablecloth. This is a shady spot that I use a lot as it is close to the house and it's just perfect for breakfast or afternoon tea. I love having tea parties; I'm much better at teas than dinners.

*Adopt the pace of
nature: her secret
is patience.*
  Ralph Waldo Emerson

A pretty Florentine gilded chest of drawers is the least scruffy of my flea-market finds, I like the fact that it makes a quite formal statement in my entry hall (*opposite*). The items piled on the Hungarian chest and on the floor are either on their way out or on their way in, part of my process of inspiration.

One day my front garden will billow with lavender, until then there's always the farmer's market for flowers (*below*).

The way in

The moment you open the front door, you get a feeling for my place, and this entry way tells everything about my house. There aren't many doors, there's a feeling of linked, flowing spaces, there are beautiful things but no clutter, there's a muted palette of old golds, pinks, and blues, a feeling of calm and the promise of comfort. It is also a very functional space. Behind the door underneath the stairs is a washing machine and in the Hungarian painted chest I keep my soap powder. The niche was a detail I loved about the house. I installed a candlelight fixture that I normally leave illuminated, which is my way of paying the household gods respect.

My good luck elephant (*below*). He did have his trunk curling under, which is bad luck. Beau, who does all my antique restoration, took him away one day, broke his trunk, and turned it around. I like the bohemian twist the elephant brings to my entryway.

The misplaced but much appreciated balcony (*right*) really belongs on a Southern mansion. The shutters were black and I repainted them a soft gray sage, a simple adjustment that made all the difference. I love nothing more than sitting quietly on my church pew in the morning, acknowledging my gratitude for the day. I am still on the lookout for the right exterior lanterns. Black is a little austere for me.

HILLTOP
LIVING

Amy's family tree house

(*previous page*) This is an indoor/outdoor room. Two pairs of double-hung doors are such a practical and dramatic feature. Brick floors are painted white and softened with cheap Chinese grass mats. The modern light fixture is still twinkly and whimsical. Florals have space, whether through art or Amy's own photography, as a hit of color on the coffee table or a frilly cloth on her Chinese shutters.

Mismatching tableware (*left*). The cement wall (*opposite*) is original to the 1950s house. Amy whitewashed it to soften the harsh concrete, making an amazing backdrop for the crystal chandelier.

Feasts and small gatherings

Amy and Shaun's house started as a little tree house. It has been recently remodeled to create an airy sweep of interconnected spaces. Amy and I have been part of each other's creative evolution: she has photographed my last four books so we have built a silent language. Her house represents to me modernity with warmth, due probably to a lot of activity in the house with two kids and a photo studio. The textures of cement, wood, and paint have an industrial, edgy feel and the comfort comes from sheepskin throws, overstuffed linen cushions, and touches of whimsy. Amy's taste is a little more modern than mine, but we share core recipes for our decorating—the common thread of beauty, comfort, function persists, with a twist. With two small boys and sticky fingers, the dining area, a farmhouse harvest table at one end of the kitchen, is no place for fragility. The chandelier, which looks so good against the crusty wall, is hung out of harm's way. Tableware is a mismatch of mercury candlesticks, old English breadboards, pastel bowls, and ivory-handled flatware and the practical chairs a mixture of scruffy white-painted wood.

(*left and below*) Velvet rosebuds on a dyed green doily: as fake as can be, but yummy. Hydrangeas can sit there for weeks, slowly drying out and changing gorgeously in texture. These sit simply in a vintage soda bottle on a rusted tin table.

(*overleaf*) When I think of Amy's house, I think of the kitchen. Amy's mother is a fantastic cook and is often to be found here cooking up delicious healthy feasts. This kitchen accounted for a major part of Amy and Shaun's remodeling budget. They wanted to capture the feel of a commercial kitchen while keeping it a happy family space with cooking and eating made practical—the concrete floors are easy for spillage and sweeping. The children's art and the red boots add real charm.

(left) A leftover hydrangea cutting.

The countertop and sink are made from concrete (*opposite*), but the baskets with endless fluffy white towels soften the scene. I find lighting is so often a problem in bathrooms whether in homes or hotels. Amy has this covered, with a pair of quirky modern light sconces on arms for flexibility.

Glamorous pampering

I always love to see how different styles can marry. In this case a very modern countertop and a vintage claw-foot tub share the space nicely. Elements from both sides keep the balance with modern and traditional bath hardware. The ethnic raspberry pink rug is a splash of femininity. The stage is set for the most glamorous bathing and pampering.

A bergere chair (*opposite*) with Bennison upholstery is probably more commonly placed in a traditional setting, but I think it handles itself quite well in its unexpected placement.

(*right*) A silken silver-blue pouch and a crumpled ribbon. It keeps Amy's fashion jewelry safe.

(*overleaf*) With all the activity in the house, I have always found Amy and Shaun's bedroom so peaceful. It is a light room with high wooden ceilings painted white, from which a tiny blue mercury glass light fixture hangs. Amy and Shaun don't worry too much about practical curtains as the house is totally private and, for now at least, August and Jackson (their boys) wake up well before sunrise.

Scrumptious accents

I always appreciate seeing items displayed in unexpected places or the marriage of different periods of design. There are several examples of this philosophy in this bathroom. A glamorous upholstered chair in a minimalist setting creates a balance of the perfect mismatch, its clean lines bringing glamour and character to a simple setting. The mixture of clean, cool, functional cabinetry and cement countertops is softened with woven storage baskets and an abundance of fluffy white towels and feminine jewelry. By staying close to the mantra of beauty, comfort, and function, the blending of most design styles can live happily and beautifully together.

"To those who can dream, there is no such place as faraway."

The white cloth cord, antique fixture, and perfect blue honeycomb mercury shade (*right*), so small but it fills the space well. Shiny bling (*left*) meets worn and treasured—a cluster of gold, silver, and glass charms dangles on a wooden knob. The opaque pink lamp base is a vintage find from the Napa valley (*opposite left*). Amy had shades made up in a silvery taupe linen that she cleverly lined with pink satin to create a lovely glow.

Whimsical sleeping

Amy has created her own style of "glamorous comfort" in a room of modern lines and high ceilings. She is a big fan of Shabby Chic bedding and has used my signature headboard in white and piled the bed with mushy pillows, wrinkly linens, and a cotton cable throw. She designed the modern book unit on one side, but I loved the way she counterbalanced it with the funky beaten-up white cupboard opposite. Once again the mix of modern and vintage demonstrates that opposites can live pleasurably together.

A spare bedroom (*below*). I love how Amy painted the brick
all white and used iridescent Moroccan blue tiles around
the fireplace. The bed with eclectic blue poplin and
linen bedding is more evidence of Amy's love of
Shabby Chic bedding.

The utility sink in the children's bathroom (*opposite*)
developed a mysterious blue stain that will not go away.
Amy has embraced the stain, as its aqua tones go well
with the other blue accents in the room.

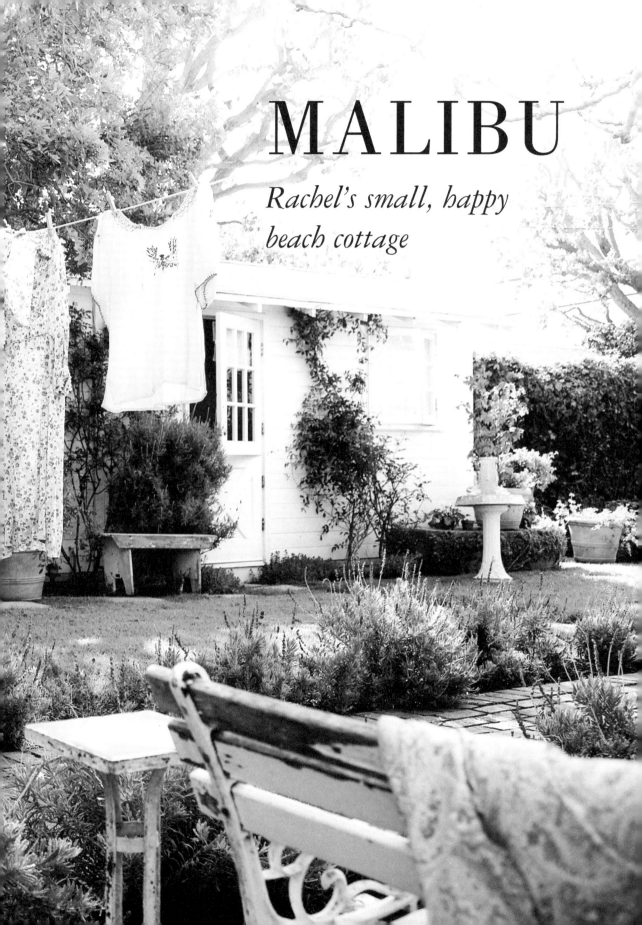

MALIBU

*Rachel's small, happy
beach cottage*

My guesthouse is my mini-barn. (*previous page*) I love the sight of washing on a line. I heard somewhere that the Victorians would plant lavender by pathways so that long skirts would brush against the plants and transfer the scent indoors.

Something special among the country rustic is the ballerina lamp (*right*). My daughter had endless sleepovers here. The queen-sized bed platform has storage underneath (*far right*).

Extra outside space

Jake and Lily's dad and I grew up in England with soggy gray playgrounds, while they had the sand, ocean, and endless sunshine of Malibu. As Jake and Lily approached teenage years I began to wonder if it would be better for us to move into "town," but the moment I moved us I realized I had made a 75 percent mistake. So within months I did my best to put things right. I bought this house out of pure desperation—it was a dump—but it has turned out to be a classic diamond in the rough. I built a guesthouse on the property, partly as a bolthole for my then-teenage daughter, who "needed some space." It couldn't be simpler, a mattress on a platform, Dutch doors, a white limestone floor you can sweep, a rug you can shake, and a fan to keep cool.

The entryway to my little house (*left*) always feels like "walking down the aisle." It can be quite tricky to create a lush garden in Malibu, due to its close proximity to the ocean, salt air, and winds, but somehow I have inherited wonderful rich soil, and lavender, roses, hydrangeas, bougainvillea, jasmine, and camellias grow here vigorously and happily. The chandelier has become a little rusty with the sea air but it adds character among the simplicity.

My lucky elephant (*right*), trunk up—as it should be for maximum good fortune—sometimes gets a welcoming candle on his back. I was fortuitous to find an elephant in shades of pastel.

(*overleaf*) The living area of my beach house is anchored with an oversized sofa slipcovered in washable white denim. Other than some gentle pastel accents of velvet decorative pillows, most everything else is white. Sand is inevitable, so everything can be swept, shaken, washed, and enjoyed.

House by the sea

It took a while for me to work out how to create the diamond from the rough. In the end I decided on a simple sunny whitewashed Greek island house with the sound of the ocean and the breeze blowing through it. It has turned out to be the most laid-back, relaxing sanctuary. A truly happy house. The house is a one-story U-shape with the path running up to the front door in the middle with the main living area beyond. The focal point is a big squashy comfort zone with slipcovers that are forgiving of sand and bare feet: an ideal space for lounging in the heat of the afternoon. No color, just lovely washed-out blending pastels. The big leather Moroccan footstool doubles as a coffee table or extra seating. The room is open plan, but I did install sliding barn doors partly for architectural interest and to give the dining area an enclosed feeling of candlelit intimacy at night.

(*previous page*) This mismatched tablesetting is my attempt to do faded elegance in a relaxed manner: pretty without being formal, and certainly not precious. I layered the chippy white painted harvest table with a patchwork of lace tablecloths, some with little imperfections. I gave new life to some tired napkins by repairing and redyeing them. I used plates from my ever-evolving collection of leftover but still lovely vintage china. Knowing a meal here could last hours, I make a special effort to have little vases of flowers so as not to interrupt reflective talk and chit chat. These dining chairs are my favorite. They are a little worse for wear now, a little ripped and a few wonky legs, but they are unlikely to get professionally repaired. However, they will live on forever as the source of inspiration for a replica chair in my Rachel Ashwell Shabby Chic collection.

My beach-house kitchen (*opposite*) is one of my favorite places to be. I am truly grateful for this home, and was pleased to find a vintage sampler (*right*) that said it for me.

Snacking and chatting

Friends wander in here, pull up a stool, and stay for hours and hours. This is a house that lends itself to gatherings, it is minimal, easy to maintain, and a pleasure to be in. The kitchen has my signature open shelving so my pretty plates and dishes furnish the room. I keep a metal bucket by the sink for tea towels and napkins, always fluffily laundered, but apart from that most things are on display. There are no built-in cabinets in this kitchen apart from the ones under the countertop that I inherited and painted in a high-gloss white. The ceiling is in a high gloss too. The kitchen surface is white Corian, hardwearing and almost indestructible. My favorite spot to perch is on the countertop to the left of the sink from where I dispense cocktails or refreshing cups of tea to friends and family seated on the bar stools.

"*The ability to simplify means to eliminate the unnecessary so that the necessary can speak.*"
Hans Hofmann

(*previous page*) This room is an overflow from the kitchen. Often a sleepy afternoon takes place right here on my Shabby Chic Bellair sofas, one of my more modern designs, but still with loose white linen slipcovers and mushy cushions. The palest pink rag rug and just a touch of pink roses was really all the color I wanted.

I love my little bathroom (*opposite*), it is beautiful, white, and functional. Perhaps a little frilly for the beach, but I wanted the silk tasseled lamp shades. Just for a little glamour.

(*overleaf*) The princess at the beach. I buy vintage clothes stands when I can, they are so useful and once hung with pretty frocks and silky nightwear, they look delicious too.

Seaside sleeping and showers

Whenever possible I like freestanding sinks with exposed plumbing in bathrooms, I like how chrome pipes look and it is reassuring knowing there is not a world of drippy moldiness hiding within a cupboard. Here I have solid functional chrome plumbing and a fine, generous sink with integral shelf. This sink is a modern repro version of the one I have at home in LA, and the faucets are new too. This is a wonderful calm space, ideal for a long soak after a salty, sandy day on the beach. I've restrained myself to tiny touches of pink: the towels, a couple of pretty jars, and the white wicker beach towel hamper with the faintest of pink stripes. I used one-and-a-half-inch hexagonal matte floor tiles to give a modern twist to a classic idea. From time to time I have rented this house. Pamela Anderson and Britney Spears have both enjoyed primping here. My bedroom is my white beach palace. The bright, reflective painted wooden floors in high-gloss white just need repainting every couple of years, which is not a big deal. I used a linen duvet cover with a dust ruffle worthy of a ball made of ruffly cotton and lace. The gold inlay on the duvet tied it all together. The chippy white painted mirror and the white wooden chair are expected in a beach house but I thought it was okay to have a touch of glamour with a mirrored dresser and a freestanding Venetian mirror. The glass blocks set high up into the wall I wouldn't choose, but I inherited them and let them be.

CELEBRITY HOMES

Hollywood and New York

(previous page) The serenity of this house is almost tangible. The walls
are of 14-inch solid concrete and have been plastered to resemble the
grain of the wood used for the ceilings.

I always like to see from one room to the next (*opposite*) but few homes
have these humble archways. Lilac is a big favorite of mine (*below left*).
I like the little ranunculuses peeping through. The faded reds of the
old book bindings (*below right*) add to the feeling of authenticity.
Cindy is a reader, so the cover is secondary to the content.

Marilyn Monroe lived here

Growing up in London, Hollywood was a faraway land to daydream
about. For me, Marilyn Monroe was a fascinating mixture of glamour
and tragedy. When I went to my friend Cindy's home, once briefly lived in by
Marilyn, I was so attracted to the quality of innocence, purity, and chapel-like calm.
Cindy and Henry Rust purchased the house in 1997 and spent 14 months deleting
additions and restoring it to its original form—a beautifully crafted Spanish hacienda.
The house still has the olive, eucalyptus, and giant corral trees planted when the
property was built in 1929.

An embroidered sampler (slightly stained) is an added blessing. The lovely
faded reds and creams are echoed throughout the house.

The main bedroom is a peaceful hideaway with the garden creeping up to it so it is screened from view. The bed is piled with vintage pillow shams and pillowcases and vintage monogrammed linen with all the connotations of lives lived and times gone by.

CURSUM PERFICIO

A tile panel at the entryway to the home (*opposite*). Cursum Perficio literally translates as "I finish the course." In this context it can be interpreted as meaning "Home at last." One of the very first inhabitants of this house was Tom Mix, cowboy star from the silent era of film who kept his horse in what was the corral at the front of the house: the motto is quite fitting for a returning horseman. The home's present owner, Cindy Rust, is the daughter of my Malibu neighbor—my Malibu mum as I call her.

White has been my favorite color forever (*below*). It is never bland though, because of the diversity of textures. As shown here, a pitcher, a stool, the textured wall, and the papery petals of white lisianthus create a tapestry of whiteness. A pretty antique Victorian pillow sham with a tiny beige ribbon—so lovely to me.

(*overleaf*) Betsy says "The kitchen is purely decorative, because I don't cook. I store things in the stove and only use it to boil water. There are lots of hooks so I can hang all my chachkas… more bobbles, bottles, bangles, beads, vases, and photos of my family and good friends everywhere: a combo of new, old, and favorite stuff. The sink is an old nickel industrial sink combined with repro Pullman car shelves. I painted my apartment super white because the space is supermodern, but sure enough I realized I can't live in white so ended up changing it to pink: cactus pink from Benjamin Moore."

Betsey Johnson lived here

Fashion designer Betsey lived in this New York apartment for 15 years. We have never actually met, but we are great fans of each other, and I have bought many of her frocks and blouses and she has bought many of my twinkles and treasures. As different as our public personas are, we both have an appreciation of pink (in different tones), lace, and pretty girly things. This is a perfect example of a different flavor of design but one that is still something I relate to. I asked Betsey about her apartment, and I think it best to let her talk about it in her own words. "The sink, vanity, and tub are old stuff I bought many years ago. I redid the bathroom (*right*) to basically show off my favorite white embroidered net curtains. I wanted it white so spray-painted the lavender glass tiles to white. I keep nothing in drawers, all the things I like to look at, bracelets, junk, and gems, are out (*above*) so I can look at them all the time. All the perfume bottles are out because I love to put on about ten different perfumes a day." It was lovely for me to learn we have so many similar philosophies. In the end, it is all about being real.

DOGS, ART, & LITERATURE

The Milches' neighborhood house

(*previous page*) Lou, oblivious to the faded prettiness and beauty of his surroundings.

Normally, I'd say a bedroom should be a calm and restful place, but I break my rules here because of what this room is busy with—an abundance of books and dogs but no anxiety (*opposite*). Phoebe surveys her territory from the sofa (*below*) and, outside on the balcony, another dog bed awaits (*left*). Cozy, floppy dog beds covered in layers of faded chinz and stripes are everywhere.

"I'm at Olivia's"

This was my son's response to my every "where are you?" call. He was always at Olivia's. This is the home of David and Rita Milch, their three children, and six very large dogs. One day I asked Rita, rather enviously, why did she think the kids gravitated toward her home? This was her reply: "I think the kids like hanging out here because it's very relaxed. They figure that in any place with six dogs you really don't have to worry about the furniture and the dogs provide entertainment. Also maybe they like that it is always the same—new paint or rug maybe—but the same furniture for 20 years. Something constant can be comforting." David is a writer and Rita an artist. They met at Yale University so their house oozes intellectual, bohemian artistry, as well as a lot of dog grooming and feeding. Everything speaks of creativity: the books are dog-eared and left about, the paintbrushes still wet, there is nothing stale or contrived.

(*previous page*) Lovely tatters. (*from left*) A delicate piece of tattered embroidered fabric on an embroidered linen pillow. A well-chewed dog leash speaks of years of love and use. Books are everywhere in this house, well-thumbed, well-read, and dog-eared. There is something poignant about things coming to the end of their lives, so while they need handling with care, they are not useless. Their frailty is something very beautiful to me.

Irregular archways lead though to the master bathroom (*opposite*). Yellow is not my favorite color, but with this exception—a sunny, warm, and faded shade with hand-painted details.

An arched mirror echoes the shape of the bathroom's eccentric openings (*right*). The wall behind is painted a lovely scrubby shade of blue.

Bohemian bathing

This is by no means a glamorous bathroom but the patinas and textures of the paint, the adventure of the nooks and archways, and the sunny but faded yellows create a lovely mini bohemian palace. The stencils around the archways, also elsewhere in the house, are by the artist Nancy Kintish. I love the silver iridescence, the way each opening has a different pattern, and the relationship between the artwork on the walls and the patchwork of Indian paintings.

(*previous page*) Olivia is truly one of the most vivacious, interested, and interesting young women I've met and with boundless energy, so it was a surprise to me that her room is as small and as peaceful as it is. The theme is blue and eclectic. The bed, angled to the window as the room is so small, is piled with Shabby Chic bedding and a vintage quilt. The wall has a collage of apparently unrelated pictures and mirrors. There's always space for a signature jug of ranunculuses and fading hydrangeas.

The uncontrived success story of Rita's layers (*right*). This is Rita's way of reupholstering an over-loved chair. I love the yellow stripes with the burgundy florals.

Disjointed and undesigned (*opposite*), welcoming layers of patterns await the pleasure of an overnight guest. A dog bed on the floor awaits—always happy to keep a guest company or vice versa.

Room for guests

Rita's decorating philosophy is to layer fabrics. If something looks a little worn or faded, it gets another layer on top. She has a happy knack of throwing together stripes and florals, paisleys and plains, and expecting them all to get along. Which they do. In this friendly space the bed is piled with patterns and, like every room in her house, it's a perfect spot to curl up. It was a very refreshing surprise for a home of this stature to have such modest-sized rooms, so for all its size, it's a cozy home.

Tableware and glasses (*left*) are mismatched flea-market finds. Jewel tones give the table a touch of theatrical attitude.

Nancy Kintish's stencils add warmth and interest (*opposite*). There is a glass of hydrangeas on the table, I just love these flowers—the way they evolve from fresh to dried, the papery texture and the faded colors, and the fact they last for a long, long time. A jug of lisianthus adds to the eclectic nature of this room.

Classy, casual dining

This is where Marie Antoinette meets Southern California. The room comfortably houses a large round table and an eclectic collection of dining chairs. It feels nicely contained. This is a proper dining room without being formal. It is a room of French doors and garden views—always a pleasure—with little touches of gilding and pretty pieces of furniture. The circular petticoat tablecloth fits in perfectly: it is made of linen and lace, it's been dyed many different colors over the years, and it never needs ironing. A frivolous table to offset the casual uniform of jeans for dinner in Los Angeles.

Formal, fun living

The endless entertaining and gatherings that take place in this house
tend to pass the living room by, but it is a confident and casual space
with a truly eclectic mixture of furniture. There are bits of California, Eastern Europe,
and France along with some maybe inherited pieces with memories. The dogs have
made their mark too, gently gnawing at chair legs and cushions so the room is neither
serious nor precious. This is as formal as this house gets, and, as Rita said, it is
relaxing to hang out somewhere that you can't do any damage. I love the faded rosy
colors, the carved mirror, and the bits of brights: the blue damask chair, and the
threadbare damask cushion.

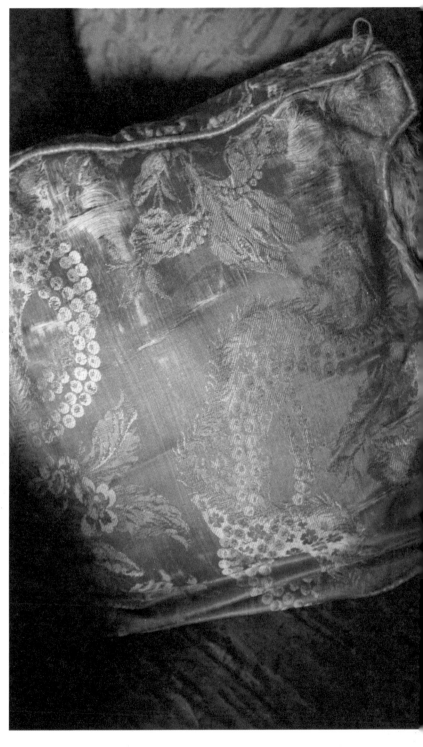

The living room (*above*) is one of the largest in a house of surprisingly small and cozy rooms. Wooden beams and rafters add to the characterful and comfortable mix.

Imperfect beauty is often the best kind (*above right*). This gorgeous, fragile damask cushion shows signs of love and age.

BEHIND THE SCENES

Design, vintage, and inspiration

I always love to catch this vision as I pass through my studio (*opposite*). The composition is of hooped, tea-stained petticoats, ballet shoes, and brocade trimming. The clothes rail shares space with my range of Rachel Ashwell Shabby Chic sleepwear. All yummy.

A prom dress on a vintage chair (*left*) with harlequin print upholstery. The unique proportions inspired me to have this chair copied.

(*overleaf, from left*) This tattered torso mannequin with its lovely silver patina was a flea-market find—to me as valid as any fine sculpture. A really large theatrical papier mâché wedding cake prop that graced the entryway of various celebrity weddings I've been asked to design. Can't get enough of a ruffle—these parasols I just love.

Backstage

My design studio is my backstage. Theatrical wardrobe departments, dressing rooms, and scenery bays have always held a fascination for me. I love the artistry that goes into building a make-believe world where the curtain rises and audiences are transported into other lives and other times. And then all the frocks and coats and shoes and ruffles, the scenery flats and furniture are piled into hampers and shipped off to the next venue for the magic to be re-created all over again. I love the way costumes and props are handmade: there's a real depth to them and I admire that they are ingeniously reused and recycled. I see a story in every costume hanging on the rail: a character, a soul—resting. I am often inspired too, when I go to the theater. I saw a recent production of the opera Otello and I came away with a vision of swirling deep orange ruffles that had a direct effect on my work.

Over the years I have collected prom dresses (*previous page*) from flea markets, vintage clothing stores, and on eBay, Mainly from the 1950s and made of cheap fabrics like satin and tulle, they are perfect to transform. I dye them, restore zippers or hooks that have seen better days, and apply floppy silk flowers or scruffy ribbons. Lastly I add stretchy gussets on the side of the bodice so they fit "normal people." I usually have some in my stores as an art installation, calling them "my traveling girls." Many have been plucked from the collection and sold, often for weddings.

My poignant Pierrot costume (*opposite*) I was told came from Paris.

One of my prom dresses (*right*), newly dyed and rosily trimmed, dances on a length of fishing wire, soon to be a "traveling girl."

Make believe

In my process of designing, soul and authenticity sit alongside my mantra of beauty, comfort, function. I like to add a light-hearted flourish: a bit of subliminal fantasy and whimsy. Theater, circuses, carnival, prom balls all inspire me. My English heritage, I think, is responsible for my fascination with circus life and the ballet. The appeal of theatrical costumes has always been very strong for me. I like to think of the joy they have given, a joy that is tinged with the inevitable sadness that the show is now over and the curtain has come down. I give these characters new life, a rebirth, and they hang there for all to see and to resonate my inspirational antennae.

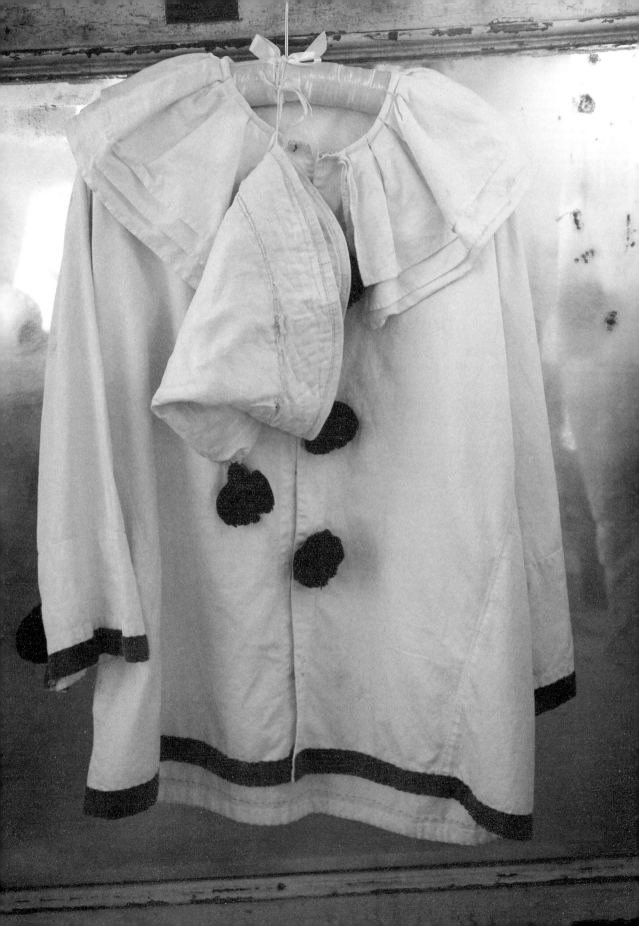

Deep talks of design. Pinned up behind me, Amy, and Angie are the season's fabric collections. The table in front of us is piled with feathers, pillows, flowers—ever-evolving tools of our trade.

Design ideas and process

I have never had formal design training. My education has been in the doing—and my doing has touched on interior design and product and fabric design. As in all design work, this has been a collaborative process. While I am very clear on my vision, I do rely on others to make my song go from mono to stereo, and that is where I need and appreciate my wonderful design team. As I articulate my vision, I learn more and more and together we create an ever-evolving body of work. I can't think of anything I've designed that hasn't been inspired by vintage. Even if I cross into contemporary territory, my signature relaxed and mushy elements still prevail. I design from the inspiration of things that interest me, not from trends. I strive for the authentic. There was a time when every fabric print had to be hand-drawn to pass on to the fabric printers. With new technology the process is much quicker but can be too perfect. We still aim for the hand-drawn attention to detail. Always looking for imperfection.

(*clockwise from left*) Behind the scenes: a silk army parachute, dyed of course, with matching pompoms—the quality of the stitchwork and tucking and the sheer artistry of this life-saving piece of flimsy fabric are an endless source of inspiration. In our office, spray paint has no regard for technology. A fabric board that will develop into a bedding collection—all yummy white with a baby blue fleur de lys. The delicate lid of a Capodimonte jewelry box has inspired all sorts of ideas.

The process of shopping is soul food to me. My warehouse (*opposite*) is full of items bursting with potential. My eye is consistent in picking out the battered creams, greens, pale powder blues, and reds that I adore.

I always keep discarded hardware from furniture and crystal drops from chandeliers (*left*). One day they will wind up as part of some other restoration.

Discovery and restoration

I grew up trailing after my parents as they haunted the flea markets of Britain: my father for antiquarian books, which were his trade, and my mother for vintage dolls that she restored and sold. This sowed the seed of my flea-market training and opened my eyes to the beauty of old, battered, and well-loved possessions. It taught me to spot things I wanted before anyone else snapped it up and it fed me with the excitement of the hunt. I only have to half-close my eyes and I can sense the anticipation, the sleepy tumble into the car well before dawn, and the anxiety of keeping up with my father's fast-moving legs as he strode through the aisles intent upon a rare find: a beautiful, valuable first edition.

While I appreciate the original function of a piece, I often find it takes only a little coaxing to turn one thing into another. Small tables can become coffee tables (I ask for forgiveness as I chop down the legs), built-in cabinets transform into nightstands, and I often swap hardware to add character. I listen to the traders tell stories of where things came from, which can sometimes be a little fanciful, but I am always happy to pass their stories along, aware that someone has fallen in love with this piece and will do so again.

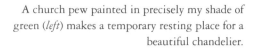

A church pew painted in precisely my shade of green (*left*) makes a temporary resting place for a beautiful chandelier.

Layered, muted colorful rugs (*below*) with tattered bindings.

I search for furniture I can either restore and use or sell, or have copied. There was a time I would paint everything white, but now I'm interested in the diversity of the original paintwork and patina, and in bringing items into my world for a clean-up, a cushion, some interesting hardware, and maybe a change of function.

A homemade doll house complete with scraps of vintage wallpaper, a tiny chandelier, and a chaise longue. Probably a little too abandoned for a five-year-old to appreciate, but I love it just the way it is: a blank canvas for designing a house or an empty stage for daydreams and dramas.

My appreciation for workmanship and the original colors of pieces I buy has only increased over time. Often the furniture I find has been made to fulfill a particular need by farmers, whose carpentry skills and traditions have been handed down through generations. I am not talking about conventional antiques that probably belong in a formal interior, but about people's furniture. My kind of antiques, my farmhouse vintage pieces, have character and speak to me far more vigorously in their battered state because they have been endlessly used. I love to find people's initials carved on the top of a table. My vintage pieces have been part of someone's everyday life, and have picked up a rich patina of human history along the way. Once they've been through my process, they will, hopefully, continue along that path.

DETAILS

Fabrics, hardware, lighting, art, patina, and vintage wallpaper are a few of my favorite elements in creating a decorative symphony, with all instruments of equal importance. The star piece is always captivating, but it is the supporting roles that bring the depth.

The big picture establishes the initial impression, but I find it's the little unique details that resonate and evoke a deeper experience of a home. I often think outside the box as to how things should be used, and I give a lot of thought to the history of an object, appreciating that a history of ownership and use expresses itself through patina. The process of gathering details is a journey in itself. The search and the stories passed on from owner to owner, all add to the quality and honor of a home. And I will often leave things as I find them, because the rips, chips, cracks, and missing pieces all add character.

Art

That is such a little word for such a vital part of life. To me, art is anything that is pretty, that can somehow be displayed and enjoyed and stimulates emotions. I grew up in an artistic home, so for me pots of paintbrushes and works in process were part of my surroundings. I enjoy watercolor, oils, pastels, and embroideries. I love landscapes and thought-provoking subjects. And I love kids' art—real artless art—because there is something so honest and explosive about it. Some art I hang on the wall, but not in a serious way. I own a little hand-me-down hammer from my mum and a plastic bag of small white nails and if that does the job, art stands a chance of being hung. If not, leaning and layering is my way. Memory boards are a mainstay (*opposite*)—a manifestation of my unfolding world: kids' photos, art, invitations, bits of tat. Uncontrived and evolving, it is an honest slice of life.

A paper bell, a tiny price tag, a carved frame. An installation.

My floral and jeweled kabob. Flowers, beads, and ribbons threaded onto wire.

I do love these little oil paintings of scenes. Very unlikely they'll ever get hung. I find affordable paintings on my travels and daydream of the artist's experience.

The skull and lacy parasol share a resting place. Thought provoking.

Kids' art: Jake's proudly initialed black and white study, Lily's spirited flowers.

I love to buy embroidery pieces, to admire the patience and artistry.

My friendly gorilla, by Jake. I smile back endlessly at this one.

Fabrics and texture

Patina and bare threads are to me evidence of a life lived to the full. Perfection I find intimidating and dull and I don't want to be the one to make the first mark and break the perfection. I don't want plastic surgery on my time-worn treasures, I want to enjoy every crack, every layer of paint, every thread that hangs. I want these elements to create the tapestry of my home. Silks, velvet, linens, and lace all cohabit if they have the same acceptance of age. Different woods can tell their own story by proudly displaying their layers of different stages of life. The end result is character that is impossible to re-create. Just like memories, it takes life, history, and time. A cupboard full of unraveled edges (*opposite*), wrinkled velvet, and florals is a treasure trove waiting to be used, either to be transformed into something else or used as a spontaneous table covering. The view is an artwork in itself.

This is a little folk table that I haven't quite found a home for yet, but I do so love the colors and the folksiness of it.

Red is a color I have had to evolve into. Dark pink, as I call it, has confidence.

Teal blue is my new favorite color. This piece sits next to my stove.

A favorite. The subdued palette is a perfect balance for a handsome floral.

Lace is unobtrusive but makes a solid statement for windows, cloths, beds.

Silk: an accent of decadence hard to achieve with other fabrics.

I like to have eclectic rugs, but always faded, tattered edges, all the better.

Lighting

While a chandelier is certainly a trademark of my decorating style, the star, I am equally passionate about the understudy role of lighting. I will live with a naked light bulb rather than install a light fixture that is less than magical. For me, along with being practical, lighting sets the mood of a home. It creates whimsy, or simplicity. I like to mix function with beauty. Dimmer switches for me are a must. In my home I have chandeliers for mood, but also brighter secondary lighting from wall sconces or small, recessed halogen spotlights. There is an array of affordable lighting to be found on eBay, and at flea markets. Usually some form of restoration is needed (by an expert for the wiring) but I like the process of adding or taking away crystals, finding new/old lampshades. A big chandelier in a little place (*opposite*). At first one could say it's a waste of a lovely fixture. To me it's pure beauty.

The canopy and chain are what is substantive. Glass shade is lovely too.

Useless pull chain, as the light is on a wall switch, but love the detail.

I don't have too many of these, but perfect for a little girl's room.

A low ceiling needs a shallow fixture. I like the visibility of the tiny light bulb.

I enjoy the little pull chain and the exposed light bulb.

Simple and clean, the brass patina and crystal beads evoke tradition.

Broken, held together by wire, but still gracing a silky shade.

Full of character and detail. An unusual shade, chippy fixture, and chain.

Japanese lady lamp with the lampshade held clear of her view.

The lovely wonky ceiling-mounted chandelier is in my office.

Pale blue teardrop crystals pull together a room of blue accents.

Curtains and window treatments

There is something rather proper about the concept of curtains. They are expensive due to the amount of fabric, and the workmanship is labor-intensive. They make a window "grown-up" and it is only in the past few years that I have had a proper curtain. Up until then I improvised with panels of fabric and thumbtacks. I still think it would be too much if every room in my house had properly made curtains, so I selected which windows needed privacy, which needed light kept out, which needed décor. Then I worked out fabrics and treatments. There is quite a hodgepodge but, as is my way, it's not a contrived hodgepodge. (*Opposite*) Silvery-pink and ruched and smocked at the top. The glamour of this room is totally credited to these curtains. The puddling where the fabric breaks on the floor is just perfect. They are lined to give a lovely weight and to muffle sound.

Old lace panels with a push pin, actually quite perfect.

A lace panel, folded over a small brass café rod. Just lovely.

Smocking and ruching and abundance on natural wood pole and rings.

A vintage banner lets in the light. Not practical for a bedroom, but pretty.

A grommeted denim curtain hangs from a metal pole with shower rings.

A baggy rod-pocket detail gone beautifully wrong.

Wooden shutters that leak light for imperfect charm.

Ring and clips placed irregularly along the top of a curtain.

Vintage wallpaper

My own private passion. Most vintage papers I find on the internet and if I love the pattern I will buy as much as I can find, sometimes 15 rolls, sometimes only one. Vintage paper is a pain to hang. Often the rolls are so old they fall apart in your hands and sometimes the edges have to be cut, as that is where the pattern name is written. They are not self-glued, so it's a six-act play to apply to the wall. But when done it's a showstopper. The old-fashioned printing has such a lovely quality. Often the paper is faded which is magical and the prints themselves are just not around today. A dream of mine is to design my own line of wallpaper with the qualities I love, perfecting the tricky elements of the true vintage. Anaglypta wallpaper (*opposite*) is a lovely material. Applying it below the high-gloss painted chair rail means I need only half the quantity of vintage.

I only found one roll of this— appreciated in my linen cupboard.

Three precious rolls became the flavor for the nook.

Faded floral paper set inside a dried- out frame. Just so nice.

You can always see the glue seam, part of the charm.

Blue roses and scrolls. The top strip is awaiting trimming.

A rose is just a rose, they say. These are perfection.

The randomness of flowers wins over linear orderliness.

Royalty china collection

I've never considered myself a collector, but gather objects to create beauty, comfort, and function and through that my life is styled. I collect lighting, rugs, art, fabrics, and everything that fills my world. In recent times I have been drawn to collecting "royalty china." I started picking up pieces for inspiration for my design work. I like the graphics, the colors: often gold embracing reds and blues. But I realize the reason I have kept going beyond my inspirational needs is my calling to heritage and home. I have been living in a foreign country for 30 years. America has been good to me but still I feel British. The process of collecting royal pieces is teaching me about my roots. The crème de la crème (*opposite*): the colors are extraordinary: raspberry, pale green, pale blue, gold and so cracked and creamy. There are 100 ideas in this little cup, celebrating the coronation of King George V and Queen Mary.

Crowns, flowers, and flags: details of inspiration for future design work.

Coronation of King Edward VII and Queen Alexandra, 1902.

I love the monochromatic blue Queen Elizabeth.

Something rather humorous about this lion.

Charmingly lopsided, a Silver Jubilee mug for King George and Queen Mary.

Serious Queen Victoria. I love the hip turquoise and red flags.

QEII: Great Queen, perfect pen pot or toothbrush holder.

Lovely quality of hand-painting: you can literally feel the paint.

Favorite things

There are numerous reasons why I consider things my favorite. It might be sentimental, it might be useful, or it might be I just love it. I have found myself becoming more and more spiritual in feeling as the years go by. This gives me reason to consider my appreciation for qualities of life. It makes me question, so I can find answers. My mum, for instance, had a lovely collection of old journals. The penmanship alone is beautiful, but so is the quality of expression. I can but wonder what the process of technology is doing to us—communicating brief thoughtless words, lost by a delete button. I try to be light in my spirit, but I know I have great passions and am a seeker for understanding. So the things that I choose to include in my favorite things are beautiful but often have a deeper meaning. I give this the perfect stage (*opposite*). To me, this is Perfection. Peace. Faith.

A tiny practical little hand holds all my jewels between her fingers.

This teeny tiny thimble and its tutu are as light-hearted as I get.

My washing machine cupboard door with gift of velvet and beads.

My mum's very happy big Buddha and the little tiny one.

One of my mum's journals: a sketchbook of true artistry.

Candles will drip where they will. And the drips get frozen in time.

Glass for protection, practicality, and prettiness. My three p's.

Favorite candles: Votivo, black currant, and Santa Maria Novella, iris.

RESOURCES

www.shabbychic.com
My website and blog

USA

Benison Fabrics
Great linen and silk fabrics (see page 97)
www.bennisonfabrics.com

Country Roads Antiques, California
Primitive flea-market finds
www.countryroadsantiques.com

Cox Paint, California
Specialists in custom-blended colors
www.coxpaint.com

Down Home Antiques, California
American Country antiques
www.downhomeantiques.com

Hannah's Treasures, Iowa
Selection of vintage wallpaper from the 1920s to the 1960s
www.hannahstreasures.com

Indigo Seas, California
Lovely, eclectic home furnishings store in LA
www.splendora.com/cityguide/reviews/los_angeles/indigo_seas/178028

Robert Ireland
The most patient contractor in the world!
Tel: 310 422 5757

Rosie's Vintage Wallpaper
Fantastic collection of vintage wallpaper
www.rosiesvintagewallpaper.com

Teleflora
USA's top flower delivery service, and supplier of all flowers in the photos here
www.teleflora.com

Yannetty Landscape
For great garden landscaping
www.yannettylandscape.com

Zoffany
Regal wallpaper (see page 45)
www.zoffany.com

MARKETS

Ann Arbor Antiques Market, Michigan
Wide range of antiques
www.annarborantiquesmarket.com

Brimfield Flea Market, Massachusetts
New England's biggest outdoor antiques fair
www.brimfield.com

eBay
The world's biggest online auction site—perfect for antique hunting
www.ebay.com

Find A Flea Market
Great site for finding local flea markets
www.findafleamarket.com

Flea USA
Gives listings by state of flea markets
www.fleausa.com

Marburger Farm Antique Show, Texas
Week-long antique shows in Texas
www.roundtop-marburger.com

Scott Antique Markets
Large shows in Atlanta and Ohio
www.scottantiquemarket.com

UK

Liberty, London
London's best home furnishing department store
www.liberty.co.uk

MARKETS

Alfie's Antique Market, London
One of London's best markets, loved by collectors across the globe
www.alfiesantiques.com

Antiques News
Great website with news on fairs
www.antiquesnews.co.uk

Portobello Road, London
The world's largest antiques market
www.portobelloroad.co.uk

Shepton Mallet Market, Somerset
Market every Friday
www.sheptonmallet.org

Swinderby Antiques Fair, Lincolnshire
One of the UK's largest antiques fairs
www.arthurswallowfairs.co.uk

The Royal Bath and West Show, Somerset
Stands include clothing, food, art, and craft plus traditional agricultural ones
www.bathandwest.com

MY FAVORITE MUSIC FOR MY HOME, WHEREVER THAT MAY BE...

Bruce Springsteen
Working On A Dream / Brilliant Disguise / The Wrestler

Bob Dylan
It Ain't Me, Babe

Mick Jagger
Old Habits Die Hard

Tracy Chapman
Baby Can I Hold You

Vince Hill
The Only Love

Charley Pride
Please Help Me, I'm Falling (In Love With You)

Merle Haggard
Always Wanting You / Today I Started Loving You Again

Joe Cocker
Let It Be

Mat Kearney
Breathe In Breathe Out

Andrea Bocelli
Time To Say Goodbye

Dusty Springfield
You Don't Have To Say You Love Me

Luciano Pavarotti
Ave Maria

Bono, Brian Eno, Luciano Pavarotti, The Edge, Dolores O'Riordan, Jovanotti, Meatloaf, Michael Bolton, Simon Le Bon, Zucchero, and Nenad Bach
Nessun Dorma

Bryan Adams and Luciano Pavarotti
All For Love / O Sole Mio

Meatloaf
For Crying Out Loud / Two Out Of Three Ain't Bad

Damien Rice
The Blower's Daughter

Righteous Brothers
Unchained Melody

Trace Adkens
You're Gonna Miss This

R.E.M.
Everybody Hurts

Jackson Browne
Sleep's Dark And Silent Gate

David Gray
This Year's Love

Lifehouse
Broken

George Strait
I Cross My Heart / Carrying Your Love With Me / The Best Day

Nickelback
Gotta Be Somebody

Neil Young
Only Love Can Break Your Heart

Rolling Stones
Wild Horses / Ruby Tuesday

Patti Scialfa
Love's Glory

The Eagles
The Girl From Yesterday

Elton John
Sacrifice

Sarah McLachlan
I Love You / Angel

John Lennon
Imagine

Snow Patrol
Chasing Cars

Sade
By Your Side

Leona Lewis
Better In Time

Emmylou Harris
Together Again

Coldplay
Fix You / The Scientist

Dido
White Flag / Stoned / Life For Rent

(right) A weathered oak table and chairs, dressed in linen seat covers, bring beauty to a raw kitchen. The grand chandelier adds another dimension.

INDEX

B hopeful, B happy, B cheerful, B kind,
B bury of Body, B modest of mind.
B earnest, B truthful, B firm & B fair,
Of all mis B haviour B sure & B ware.
B think ere you stumble for what
you B fall,
B true to yourself & B fruitful to all.

B brave to B ware of sins that B sets
B sure that one sin will another B get.
B watchful, B ready, B open, B frank,
B polite to all what-ever the rank.
B just & B generous, B honest, B wise,
B mindful of time & B certain it flies.

B prudent & B liberal of order B fond,
B uy what you need B fore Buying Beyond
B prompt, & B dutiful yet still B polite
B grateful B cautious of those who B tray
And truly B loved thou shalt B
B lieve me to B
your B loved friend
D.T.
March 1904